OPTIONS TRADING

STRATEGIES

The Ultimate and Complete
Guide on How to Make Money
with the Best and Working
Options Trading Strategies to
Generate a Long-Term Passive
Income and Quit Your Job

RONALD EMPHIT

TABLE OF CONTENTS

Introduction

Here we are back at it again! In this fifth section of the course, we are going to be digging deeper into options trading. We will be putting into practice what we learned so far and even taking it a step further. In this section, we will explore more step-by-step examples, using the strategies we have already learned and really showing a full-fledged strategy that is capable of fitting the market conditions, the sector you are looking to break into, and your investment budget.

Let's take a rapid look back at some of the things you should have in place by this point. You should have the desire to get started in investing; you will have made the decision whether to invest in stocks or options and your reasoning as to which is better for you and why. For some it is going to be a money issue, how much do you either have or want to put into the market. This is because some brokerages and methods of trading will require you to have a minimum account balance (remember we talked about this in the previous section where we discussed the difference between swing and day trading).

After deciding those aspects, then you will have opened your brokerage account and started formulating your initial investment strategy, this might have already evolved a couple of times based on what we've learned so far, and that is totally fine. As the markets change, so does your investment plan sometimes. You don't have to stay committed to one strategy for the rest of your life. And then, you may have even exercised a few trades by the time we reach this point. And congratulations if you have! Welcome to the big show. It's time for you to fly, fledgling investor.

In this portion of the course, the series of strategies we are going to talk about have been briefly touched upon before, but with some new elements introduced, we will see how these strategies fit seamlessly into your investment toolbox. Getting towards the end of this section there are new strategies that we haven't discussed because, at first glance, they can seem really intricate and intimidating, which is why we have saved them from going over during these last two sections in order to give you a chance to get your footing with options and to build your confidence. That being said, these newly introduced strategies, while more complicated than any other we've worked with before, are invaluable to formulating the perfect approach to make those big moves and build your portfolio. We will end up moving up another notch with the final section and our most advanced strategies yet. But for now, let's just focus on these new and old friends.

So are you pumped? Let's take the next to last step in solidifying your goals and making your options trading dreams a reality.

Chapter 1
Overview on Strategies

So, it's no secret that there are as many variations of options trading strategies as there are stars in the Milky Way. And these strategies are not one-size-fits-all... not every strategy is going to work for every situation or every investor. That's why we are going to talk about a lot of different strategies so you can see the benefits and limitations of each. You expected me to say we are going to give you options to try out, weren't you? See, I missed a great pun opportunity there. I mean, you should be dancing up and down. I rarely pass up such an opportunity. But here we go!

Wheel Strategy

The wheel strategy is probably my most utilized strategy lately. So we will spend some time taking this one a step at a time. First off, let's talk about what this strategy Is, and then we'll work our way up from there.

Basically, the wheel strategy is a plan designed to sell puts and covered calls all as a part of an investor's long-term strategy. Some people in the industry even utilize this approach as a way to generate a monthly income. Basically, the strategy boils down to this:

– You first sell CSP options on an underlying asset until you get assigned and receive the shares of stock.

– Your next step is that you will want to sell the covered call option on the underlying stock until it is swept away, and then you would need to sell the shares

– rinse and repeat like your favorite shampoo.

Sounds pretty straightforward, right? I wish I could say it was as easy as it sounds if we are just being honest here. Basically, the thinking behind it is that you sell your CSPs multiple times to collect the option premium. Here's where a lot of traders hit a snafu. If you ever get assigned, you do have to buy the stock at the agreed price. This isn't a big deal, but it's something to keep in mind because it can and will happen at some point...next while holding the stock, you want to sell covered calls on it in order to receive another premium. Once your stock is swept away, you are required to sell the shares, and then you can repeat the process to sell more puts on the same or completely different stock.

This strategy will almost certainly pan out when you decide to exercise a long position. This strategy will also allow you to rake in the dividends and make gains from the appreciation of the stock price all the while you are hanging onto the stock shares, and then it will finally pay you once more when you finally close the position.

We are going to deconstruct this strategy like a choose your own adventure book. We will start with the step and then include some examples to help make the process completely transparent and easily navigable. Without further adieu, let's start with step 1.

Step 1:

First things first, the strategy starts where many strategies do, and that's with a sale. You are going to sell a put option on a stock and collect the premium, which is a good first place to start, right? An idea to keep in mind is that you will want to select stocks that you have researched and are feeling confident to buy if it lands at a specific price. You will eventually have to hold onto them for the long term. When the put option meets its expiration date, there are two potential outcomes one might expect to see.

Outcome 1: the stock price is rising above the strike price. If this happens, the option becomes worthless when it expires, and you can retain 100% of the premium you collected when selling the option. Basically, you are receiving money to be willing and able to buy one of your already researched stocks at the price you set out and agreed upon at the option expiration date. It would be a great idea then to move on and begin to find new puts on the horizon to trade.

Let's look at a bright example to see how this all plays out...Verizon is trading at one hundred dollars per share, and I decide to sell one put option contract that has a $95 strike price with a 30-day expiration date. I would end up receiving a total premium of $300 ($3.00 x 100 if you remember now, the premium is set up). When the 30 days are up, the stock is currently trading at $96, which is above the strike price. In this particular situation, the option would expire worthlessly, and I would be able to keep the entire $300 premium. In essence, my trade would be profitable even if the stock dipped in price over the contract's time frame. The result would still come out the same if the stock at expiration was trading at any price that was higher than the strike price.

Outcome 2: the stock price dips below the strike price. For this case study, for every option you hold, you would be required to purchase 100 shares of the stock at the specified strike. That wouldn't be a problem since I thought this trade would be bullish given the stock anyway, and I was now buying it at a steal since the price was lower than what it was when I sold the put option. Also, given the circumstances, I would be able to keep the full premium that I collected initially, thereby lowering the overall cost of the underlying stock, which is music to my ears.

Now let's check an example of how this outcome works, we'll stick with Verizon here as our stock...and it is currently trading at one hundred dollars. I was able to sell one put contract that had a $95 strike price, 30-day expiration date, and would allow me to collect a total premium of $30. After 30 days had passed the stock was trading at $94, so it had dipped below the strike price. In this event... once we reach the expiration date, I was selected, and now I am required to buy a hundred shares of the underlying stock at the strike of $95 even if it is currently trading at a market price of $94.

Also, since we are just sitting here talking, you get to keep the full premium, and that would automatically reduce the cost basis of the stock itself. But then the thing becomes that you bought the stock at $95, and the additional premium of $3 per share (which came about after selling the put option) factors in further reducing the overall cost basis down to just $92. So if I go ahead and want to sell the stock while it is trading at the market price of $94, I would still end up with a profit of two dollars per share, which is a tidy sum for a beginner trader.

Putting Step 1 All Together—Example

Back to our example, Verizon is trading a hundred bucks a share, and I want to sell one put contract that has a $95 strike price, a 30-day contract, and collecting a total premium of $300 ($3.00 x 100). Once we reach the expiration date, the stock is trading at $89, which is well below the strike price. If this happens, I would be allocated and would be required to purchase a hundred shares of stock at the strike of $95 even though that it has a current market price of $89. Not to mention in this example, I would be able to keep the full three-hundred dollar premium, which would allow me to lower the cost of the stock price further.

Still good so far? So with the three-dollar premium per share (which I received from selling the put option) wouldn't give me the ability to protect myself from the price depreciation of the stock. This time with the total cost of $92 being above the market price of $89, and if I decided I wanted to get rid of the stock immediately, I would have ended up with a loss of three bucks per share. But last but not least, I could hang onto the stock and then wait for the trend to reverse itself. Since I was bullish on the stock (you can tell this back when I sold the initial put option), that shouldn't be much of an issue unless some inexplicable events changed my overall outlook about the stock.

But here's the plot twist. I think the stock is going to keep dropping, so I decide there is still time to sell the shares and accept the forfeiture. No matter which way you go, the capital you are forced to forfeit on this specific trade would be mitigated by using the Wheel Strategy than if you had bought the stock at its original price of a hundred dollars. No matter which side of the debate you find yourself on, this strategy is an excellent idea to help lower the overall cost of the stocks you like and are looking to buy regardless.

Step 2:

When you happen to be assigned a stock, then you want to sell an OTM-covered call that has a strike that is higher than what it currently costs. If the stock rises in price, but the covered call is not considered ITM upon its end date, then you would still be able to glean a profit from the collecting the premium and the collection of other capital gains that are beyond the entry price.

So during the time you are holding onto the shares of the underlying security, you are able to generate additional income by selling covered calls multiple times to bank more premiums. This part of the strategy will also mitigate the cost of the stock just to prevent the worst-case scenario in which all of these options end up expiring valueless. The investor can keep repeating the process until the stock hits ITM before its end date, and the shares get carried away.

Traditionally you would want to avoid selling this type of option if the strike is lower than its cost, as that would count as being unprofitable in the overall trade. To prevent this from happening, you will certainly have to keep track of each of the premiums plus the stock appreciation value.

There might be times when you get caught hanging onto the stock for an extended time frame until the trend resumes so you can achieve a higher range of profitability. For this reason, it's important to pick stocks that you are fine with potentially owning for the long run.

This cycle generally ends when the stock shares are called away from you, as we have discussed before.

In the case of trading dividend stocks, it is

possible to possess the shares long enough to gain some dividends. For this reason, the Wheel is able to generate an additional source of income, so if we are keeping count, through the cycle, you would have gained a premium from selling the CSP and the covered calls, as well as any dividends you might have received while hanging onto the shares. Finally, perhaps you can also reap some capital gains on the stock price.

Putting the Wheel Together

Back to our example: so, Verizon is currently trading at a hundred dollars per share, and I decide to sell a CSP contract that has a $95 strike price, thereby gaining a premium of three hundred dollars. On the expiration date, Verizon is trading at $96, which is higher than the strike price. For this example, the option will expire worthlessòy and I end up keeping the three hundred dollar premium.

Next, I am going to sell a put option on Verizon that will have a $90 strike price, and in this instance, I gain a premium of two dollars per share. On the expiration date, Verizon is running at $88, which is lower than the strike. I manage to get assigned, and then I buy a hundred shares at the $90 strike per share. This happens even if the stock is currently trending below that price.

After I buy my assigned shares, Verizon keeps trending down for 3-4 weeks, and when the price is holding at $84, I decide it's time to sell a covered call that has a strike of $87, and then I collect a two-dollar per share premium. When that expires, Verizon is still trading at $84, so the option expires valueless, and I would keep the premium.

The following step would be to start a new covered call that has a $86 strike price and gaining a three-dollar premium for each share. When this one expires, Verizon is trading at $87, so my shares are called away, and I have to sell my shares at the agreed-upon $86. In this instance, I get to keep the full premium.

And lucky me, while I am hanging onto my Verizon shares, I receive a dividend of a dollar for each of my shares.

So let's run the numbers here:

We get the dollar per share for the dividends, then the three bucks for each share on the second covered call, and we'll add to that the two dollars per share for the first covered call, and finally our three dollars per share for the CSP. This gives us a total of $11 for each share.

So, in this step-by-step example, we see that we were buying Verizon at $90, and the shares sold at $86 per share; this left us losing four bucks on each share. But the silver lining was that the total premium we gained made us able to offset the depreciation of price and still left us with a profit of $7.00 per share by utilizing this strategy.

Final Thoughts on the Wheel

You see after our breakdown that this strategy definitely has its merits, but it's also not without its risks. There are a few things that could potentially go wrong and cause a potential loss, but that's a potential outcome with a lot of options and strategies. This one is pretty close to one of the ones that even when market conditions try and affect your trade, there are some safety valves built into, even if you lose. You can still potentially make a profit.

Calling the Bulls

The next strategy we are going to delve into is

the bull call spread. This strategy combines a long lower strike price call and a short higher strike price call, and they share the same end date. It's a gamble that the underlying stock will climb, but it might not rise above the strike price of the shorter call. This strategy would cap the potential upside in return for higher gains over that by just buying a call. Using the longer call would give you a layer of protection for your portfolio in case the short call goes wrong.

Let's lay out a quick example here...so let's say that Target is trading at $50 per share, and there is a call option for $5 available that has a $50 strike and the expiration date is in 6 months. Then there is a $60 call option that has the same end date, and will be able to be sold for two dollars. Here's how everything shakes out with this strategy.

	A	B	C	D
1	Stock Price at Expiration	$50 Long-Call Profit	$60 Short-Call Profit	Bull-Call Spread Profit
2	$80	$2,500	-$1,800	$700
3	$70	$1,500	-$800	$700
4	$60	$500	$200	$700
5	$55	$0	$200	$200
6	$53	-$200	$200	$0
7	$50	-$500	$200	-$300
8	$40	-$500	$200	-$300
9	$30	-$500	$200	-$300
10	$20	-$500	$200	-$300
11				

Figure 24: Table – the bulls

A good follow-up question is, what are the upsides to using this particular strategy? One point is that it costs less capital to set up, it would reduce the breakeven point, it gives you a better return up to the short strike, and it would reduce your potential downside.

The Bear

In options trading, we like to embrace our animal side. The bear put spread is up next on our list of the more advanced strategies. At first glance, you might possibly think this looks a lot like the bull call spread, and you would be correct, except for a couple of key differences. The first would be that it's a gamble on the slight decline of a stock instead of betting on the rise. This strategy units a long higher price strike put along with a short lower price strike put. This strategy forecasts that the stock will take a dip, perhaps not much below the lower strike price, but it will still fall. This type of strategy would cap the potential upside in return for a higher profit percentage than just purchasing a put option.

Here's how this one works: Apple is trading at fifty bucks per share, and there is a put contract with a $50 strike for $5, and it has an end date that's in six months. There is also a $40 put available with the same end date, and it is $2. Here's how this one looks:

	A	B	C	D
13	Stock Price at Expiration	$50 Long-Put Profit	$40 Short-Put Profit	Bear Put Profit
14	$80	-$500	$200	-$300
15	$75	-$500	$200	-$300
16	$60	-$500	$200	-$300
17	$55	-$500	$200	-$300
18	$50	-$500	$200	-$300
19	$47	-$200	$200	$0
20	$45	$0	$200	$200
21	$40	$500	$200	$700
22	$30	$1,500	-$800	$700
23				

Figure 25: Table – The bear

So why is this option a good one? It costs less to set up, much like the bull-call spread. It lowers your potential downside, gives you a better return, and finally raises your breakeven point.

Going Long

Our next strategy is the long straddle, and this strategy pairs an ATM long call along with an ATM long put with the same expiration and the exact same strike. With this particular strategy, it speculates that a stock will experience significantly higher or lower trends, but you won't be able to call exactly which direction things are going to go.

Let's go a little deeper here. With this strategy, Wal-Mart stock is trading at $50 for each share. In this instance, there is a call and a put available, there is a $50 strike on each and they are available for $5. The end date is in six months. Here's how the numbers look with this strategy.

	A	B	C	D
25	Stock Price At Expiration	$50 Call Profit	$50 Put Profit	Long-Straddle Profit
26	$80	$2,500	-$500	$2,000
27	$70	$1,500	-$500	$1,000
28	$60	$500	-$500	$0
29	$55	$0	-$500	-$500
30	$50	-$500	-$500	-$1,000
31	$45	-$500	$0	-$500
32	$40	-$500	$500	$0
33	$30	-$500	$1,500	$1,000
34	$20	-$500	$2,500	$2,000
35				

Figure 26: Table – going long

So why does this one work? This one is gonna cost you, and that is why you would typically not pull this strategy out of your investment toolbox unless you expect a big price shift, but you can't tell which way the stock might turn. For our purposes here, the numbers show that the breakeven is right around twenty percent above or below the original stock price. That's a pretty big molehill to climb over when establishing a long straddle, but that kind of dramatic shift can happen in a sector like biotech, where the release of test results could cause a tumultuous jump in a stock of 50% or more over the course of the trading day.

The Long Strangle—Not a True Crime Podcast

So like with some other strategies and their seeming doppelgänger, this strategy resembles another that we have talked about, which was the long straddle, but here we are combining a long call along with a long put. They both have the same expiration date; here's where there's a difference. This strategy utilizes OTM options instead of ATM options. A shared characteristic of the long straddle, this strategy bets on the fact that the underlying stock will significantly trend either higher or lower, but the person looking to invest is unsure of which direction things will head. One perk of this strategy is that it is a lot cheaper to set up than the long straddle because this strategy uses OTM options, but it requires more dramatic price shifts, either higher or lower, to make this a profitable endeavor.

As a quick example, let's just say that shares of Sony are trading at $50 for a single share. A call option with a $60 strike is $2, and there is also a put with a $40 strike for $2, and both contracts have an end date that is six months out. Here's how the figures look for.

	A	B	C	D
37	Stock Price At Expiration	$60 Call Profit	$40 Put Profit	Long Strangle Profit
38	$80	$1,800	-$200	$1,600
39	$70	$800	-$200	$600
40	$64	$200	-$200	$0
41	$60	-$200	-$200	-$400
42	$55	-$200	-$200	-$400
43	$50	-$200	-$200	-$400
44	$45	-$200	-$200	-$400
45	$40	-$200	-$200	-$400
46	$36	-$200	-$200	$0
47	$30	-$200	$800	$600
48	$20	-$200	$1,800	$1,600
49				

Figure 27: Table – long strangle

So when would you use this one? This strategy is another one where the investor forecasts that the stock will shift a significant amount, but they aren't sure in which direction. This strategy is quite aggressive over the long straddle. One thing to be said, about, it though is that it is significantly cheaper. The wider range of the strike requires that the underlying stock has to move even more dramatically in order for the strategy to break even. But, once that gateway has been breached, the gains pile up even quicker than the straddle's would. Since the strangle's OTM contracts, make it cheaper to set up, the potential of losing your shirt on it if things go wrong is more significant.

Synthetic Moves

The final strategy we are going to go over in this chapter is the synthetic long...this strategy integrates a long call and a short put which share the exact same end date and strike price. The thinking behind this one is to clone the upward trend of actually owning the underlying stock.

For this strategy to function, the returns from

selling the put will counterbalance the cost of the call, and it's possible for investors to have to put up very little net investment. There are some more aggressive synthetic longs out there and they can be established with a strike price, which is higher than the current stock price, but on the other hand, there are more conservative forms of this strategy that are established below the stock price.

Back to an example of how this would be structured. Coca-Cola is trading at fifty dollars per share. There are both a call and put contract with a $50 strike available for $5; both contracts have an end date six months out. Here's how the profits would look in this strategy.

	A	B	C	D
51	Stock Price At Expiration	$50 Call Profit	$50 Put Profit	Synthetic Long Profit
52	$80	$2,500	$500	$3,000
53	$70	$1,500	$500	$2,500
54	$60	$500	$500	$1,000
55	$55	$0	$500	$500
56	$50	-$500	$500	$0
57	$45	-$500	$0	-$500
58	$40	-$500	-$500	-$1,000
59	$30	-$500	-$1,500	-$2,000
60	$20	-$500	-$2,500	-$3,000
61				

Figure 28: Table – synthetic moves

So when would you use this strategy? This particular strategy can be useful if you are looking to have the performance of a stock without having to invest that level of capital. The trade-off is that the investor must be willing and able to purchase the stock if it drops below the strike price at its expiration date.

Final Thoughts

This will be the first chunk of the strategies you will be seeing mentioned on a lot of the YouTube videos, Facebook groups, and some research/strategy sources. There are a few others that we will discuss later on in this section because they are a little more involved. They are going to require a whole chapter on their own in order to make sure we discuss them in adequate detail. But for now, I would go ahead and familiarize myself with these strategies and try them out. The simulators we discussed earlier in the course are pretty much my favorite to try out these more complicated strategies. The ones with a lot of moving parts and multiple trades you have to orchestrate are usually the ones you will want to practice before just jumping into the deep end of the pool.

The one thing I will certainly say is that these strategies, while they are a little more complicated than some of the others we have discussed before, but nothing is insurmountable. Don't think that this is something you can't figure out, and it takes time and experience to get comfortable trading options. Despite all the years I've spent trading, I still sometimes second guess myself; it's just part of it. So don't think that you are falling behind or that investing isn't for you. I's a learning curve.

Chapter 2

Protecting Against the Black Swan

There are all of these books that try to help you prepare for the worst-case scenario in all sorts of situations. But what do you do when the worst-case scenario hits your portfolio? There are things that you can do to mitigate the impact amongst your investments. So in case of emergency, break glass or just keep reading and we will help guide you through.

What is a Black Swan Event?

So that's one of those things that are just murmured about in investment circles. It's like that infamous wizard that shall not be named, and these events are treated about the same way! But the basic definition of a black swan is an unpredictable event that goes above and beyond what you would normally await to see happening and could have potentially severe consequences.

These events are typically characterized by their rarity, the severity of the impact they can have on the financial markets, and the widespread belief that they were obviously happening in hindsight.

Understanding the History

This term was first being passed around after renowned finance professor Nassim Nicholas Taleb discussed the phenomenon in his book that was published in 2007 and gained in popularity during the 2008 financial crisis. Taleb argued that these types of events are practically impossible to be able to predict because of their extreme rarity, yet they can have catastrophic consequences. He went on to add that it is important for people always to assume a black swan is a distinct possibility, no matter where it might emerge from, and it is essential to plan accordingly. Some investors are a strong proponent of the belief that having a well-diversified portfolio may offer some level of protection if a black swan event should occur. For this reason, we have advocated early on in this course about diversifying your portfolio and making sure you explore all of the different investment opportunities as well as the different sectors you can trade-in. Taleb later went on to use the 2008 financial crisis as a prime example of furthering his theory regarding black swan events and potentially how if a broken system is allowed to fail. It may strengthen it against the destruction that might happen during future black swan events. The fascinating part of his theory was that he argued that if a system that is continually being propped up and keeping it isolated from risk ultimately makes the system more vulnerable to a catastrophic loss in the face of unpredictable events.

According to Taleb, three aspects must be met before a situation will be considered as a black swan event.

The event is so rare that even the possibility that it might occur is unknown.

It would have a major impact if it happened to occur.

It's explained afterward as it was actually predictable.

Special Considerations

As far as these events go, Taleb makes the point that the standard instruments of probability and prediction, such as normal distribution, do not apply in these circumstances because they are contingent on a large population size. The past sample sizes are never accessible for rare events by definition. Using these data points that are based on observations of events that happened in the past is not accommodating for pinpointing when a black swan might take place, and it might even make us more at risk to them.

The last key facet of a black swan is that since it is considered a historically significant event, those who took part in it are racing to explain it later after the fact, and then they want to postulate on how it could have been predicted and prevented. Such speculation does not actually aid in predicting future black swan events. These events can often be anything from a credit crisis being announced all the way to a war.

So when one of these types of events happens, it usually takes the form of a stock market crash that exceeds six standard deviations making it exceptionally rare from a layman's standpoint.

Historical Examples of Black Swan Events

Looking at the most catastrophic and global

events in most recent history, the crash of the housing industry in the United States that took place during the 2008 financial meltdown is probably one of the most recent and well-studied black swan events. And there were just a few pieces of evidence, even now looking back, that were even able to predict it was going to happen when it did.

2008 was a bad year for the appearance of black swan events. Zimbabwe experienced the ultimate case of inflation the world had ever seen, with an inflation rate of more than 79.6 billion percent. When an inflation level rises to that amount, it is pretty much impossible to predict and can ruin a country financially really without even trying.

Another instance was the once successful hedge fund named Long-Term Capital Management before it was dismantled in 1998 as a result of the ripple effect that was caused by the Russian government's default upon its debt, and that was definitely something that the computer models of the company could not have seen coming.

A more recent event would be the arrival of COVID-19 on the scene and the arrival of a global pandemic that disrupted markets and economies worldwide.

Chapter 3
Nothing like a Spread

We touched upon the fact of combining more than one strategy earlier when we talked about some of the new strategies that bumped up our level of difficulty from those we first learned about when we first started this course. I want to make sure we get a strong understanding of how cobbling these strategies together will help increase your options' trading prowess.

This is pretty straightforward. A combination is any options strategy that includes more than one option type, expiration, or strike price on the same underlying stock. Those in the financial sector tend to use combinations for a wide variety of strategies because they can be fine-tuned in order to produce specific payoffs that will fall into place with the individual's risk comfort level and their expectations for the current market climate.

These strategies can be pinpointed to take advantage of or prevent certain situations, so pinpointing changes in volatility or minimizing time decay are key focus points of these different strategies.

We will explore a few more building blocks here that I think are essential to understanding how these things have the ability to all fit together.

Spreads

The first one of these we are going to discuss is the vertical spreads. These involve the buying and selling of contracts of the same type but that have different strike prices. There are also horizontal and calendar spreads which is something we will discuss in just a little bit. But investors will usually choose to use a vertical spread if they are expecting a moderate move in stock price. These are directional plays and can easily reflect the investor's particular point of view...as in if they are feeling bearish or bullish with a certain stock.

So a common vertical spread would be a bull-call spread or a bull-put spread, or on the bearish side of things, the bear-call spread or the bear-put spread.

Calculating the Vertical Spread

Here are the various formulas in order to help give you an easy frame of reference as to how we get these numbers in regards to profit and loss.

Let's start with the puts:

The Bear Put: your max profit is equal to the range between the strike values on the options, this is referred to as the premium paid. Your max loss = premium paid. And the breakeven point is = the long put's strike price - premium received.

The Bull-Put: your max profit is = premium received. The max loss = the range between the strike prices - the premium received. Finally, your breakeven point = short put's strike price - premium received.

And now for the calls:

The Bear Call: your max profit is = the premium received. Your max loss = the range between the strike prices - the premium received. And the breakeven point = the short call's strike price + premium received.

The Bull Call: your max profit is = the spread between the strike prices - premium paid. Your max loss = premium paid. Finally, the breakeven point = the long call's strike price + premium paid.

Example—Vertical Spread

Here we are looking at a bullish vertical spread, so an investor friend of mine buys a contract on Meta, whose stock is currently trading at fifty dollars per share. My friend buys an ITM option that has a strike price of $45 for $4, and then they sell an OTM call with a strike price of $55 for $3.

On its expiration date, Meta's stock is going for $49 for each share. For this example, my friend would choose to exercise their call, therefore paying $45 and then turning right around and selling for $49, ending up with a $4 profit. The call contract my friend sold ends up expiring worthless.

Running the numbers, we take the $4 profit we made from the sale of our stock, add to that the $3 premium and the last step is to minus the $4 premium that they paid, which equals a net profit of three bucks for the spread.

Horizontal/Calendar Spread

This one is a common strategy that possesses the characteristics of entering a long and short position on the same underlying stock and at the same exact time, but they will have different delivery dates.

How these typically work is that an investor would purchase a longer-term option and go short a closer-term option that has the same strike price. Here's something important to note, though. If there are two different strike prices for each month, it would then be known as a diagonal spread.

There are few different names for calendar spreads. They are also often referred to as time spreads, intra-market, or horizontal spreads.

If you are considering moving forward with this strategy, there are some important things to keep in mind here. Essentially, you want to sell the close-term buy or call. Then you will want to purchase the longer-term buy or call. And it's not required that the implied volatility is low, it would be nice...don't get me wrong. But it's not a requirement for the trade to go through.

Things to Keep In Mind

The purpose of this strategy is to be able to profit from time ticking by or an increase in implied volatility in what is normally a directionally neutral strategy.

But, since we already predetermined that the goal is to be able to glean a profit from either time or volatility, the strike price needs to be as close to the underlying stock's price as possible. This spread shows how soon and long-dated options react when the time and volatility values shift around. If there is an increase in volatility, but all the other variables stay the same, that would produce a positive impact because options with a longer-term are more responsive to shifts in volatility because if you remember your Greeks, this implies a higher vega. The only thing is that the two contracts will more likely than not trade at different volatilities. That's just the nature of the markets.

Now with the passage of time, and all variables staying the same, that would also have a significant impact on the strategy if it happened at the starting point of the strategy until the shorter contract expires. After that, the strategy is only considered a long call where the value dissipates the more time elapses. Basically, as an option's pacing in regards to time decay, or theta, increases as its end date gets closer.

With this being classified as a debit spread, the maximum loss variable would be the amount paid for the purposed action. The contract that is sold is closer to its end date and would be cheaper than the option purchased, gleaning a net debit.

The suitable move to gain a profit would be to look for a stable to moderately declining underlying stock price in the course of the lifetime of the near-term option that is followed up with a strong shift during the lifespan of the long-term contract, or either a sharp trend upward in implied volatility.

When the end date of the near-term contract rolls around, the most you could gain would only come about when the underlying stock is sitting right at or even floating under the strike price of the soon to be an expired option. If the asset were trading at a higher price, then the soon to be expired option would possess some intrinsic value. However, when the near-term option ends up expiring worthless, the investor is left with an uncomplicated long call position, which would have no cap on its potential profit.

This all boils down to working best in this situation, a trader with a bullish long-term outlook would be able to reduce the cost of buying a longer-term call option.

Example of a Calendar Spread

So for the purpose of this example of a calendar spread, let's just say that it's mid-January, and Boeing stock is currently trading at $89.05. I want to open the following calendar spread:

I want to sell the February 89 contract for $0.97.

Then I want to purchase the March 89 call for $2.22.

Which makes the total cost of the spread as 2.22 - 0.97 = $1.25 and would come out to be $125 for the traditional 100 shares one commits to in most options contracts.

This particular spread will pay off higher if shares of Boeing remain somewhat stable until February's options close out, allowing the investor to collect the premium for the option that was sold.

Then, if the stock ticks upward sometime between February and the March end date, the second leg of this particular trade will produce a profit. Our ideal market shift would be for the price to show more volatility sooner in order to secure a profit, but to rise, eventually closing just below 95 on the February expiration date. This would allow the February option to expire completely worthless and would allow the investor to profit from any upward trends all the way up to the expiration date in March.

As I had mentioned before, since this is considered a <u>debit spread</u>, the maximum loss you might accrue would be just the amount paid for the strategy. The contract sold is closer to the end of its lifecycle and would possess a lower price than the option bought, producing a net debit. For the sake of this case study, the investor wants to achieve an increase in the worth associated with a rising price up to but not exceeding $95 between when I first bought the option and the February expiration date.

So what does all this mean? Let's break this example down to help us see the inner workings of this strategy. Let's say that if the investor were to rush out and buy the March expiration, the cost would have come out to be around $222 dollars, but by utilizing this strategy, the capital needed to make and hold the trade was only $125, making the trade shape up to be one of greater margin and less risk. I perceive to speak for you, but the less risk, the better in my opinion. So it is dependent upon which strike and contract style you might select. This strategy is often utilized to bring in a profit from an extensive variety of market trends.

Diagonal Spreads

The last spread we need to talk about right now would be the diagonal spread. This is really just a fine-tuned calendar spread involving two options contracts with different strike prices. This works by entering into both a long and short position on two options of the same type (either a call or put). Though these two contracts are of the same type, they each will have their own strike price as well as their own expiration date.

Because there are two aspects for each different option, that's the strike price and the end date, in the great big world of options trading, there is a myriad of different diagonal spreads.

It's generally accepted that most diagonal spreads would be a long spread and the only requirement is that the investor buys the option with the more extensive end date and then would sell the option that has the sooner expiration date. This is also an indicator for <u>call</u> diagonals and <u>put</u> diagonals alike. But like with most things, the opposite is also required. In the case of a short spread, it would require that the investor purchase the contract with the shorter expiration and would then sell off the contract with the longer expiration.

I have only one single question, how do you as an investor decide whether a long or short strategy is considered bullish or bearish? The answer to that one would be the combination of strike prices. The graphic below sets out the possibilities:

Diagonal Spread	Diagonal Spread	Nearer Expiration Date	Longer Expiration Date	Strike Price 1	Strike Price 2	Underlying Assumption
Calls	Long	Sell Near	Buy Far	Buy Lower	Sell Higher	Bullish
	Short	Buy Near	Sell Far	Sell Lower	Buy Higher	Bearish
Puts	Long	Sell Near	Buy Far	Sell Lower	Buy Higher	Bearish
	Short	Buy Near	Sell Far	Buy Lower	Sell Higher	Bullish

Figure 29: Diagonal spreads

Final Things to Consider

As you can see from our discussion, a combination often is constructed from a myriad of strategies. This is true in the case of simple combinations of two options (collars) as well as for difficult straddle and strangle strategies. More advanced plans include trading up to four different options of two different types, as is common in an iron condor spread which we will go into detail about later. With these more technical strategies, you are able to hone your risk and reward profiles in order to profit from more minute shifts in the underlying stocks price.

The biggest con, in my opinion, when you are exploring the pros and cons of some of these more complex strategies would be the increased commission cost. It is imperative for any investor to have a firm understanding of their broker's or brokerage firm's commission structure to make sure it is financially feasible to trade these complicated combinations.

There is also something to keep in mind. Some professional traders tend to use a lot of these combinations because the trades could potentially capture risk premiums, all the while safeguarding their capital from perceived risk.

When preparing to exercise a trade with an underlying stock, the investor has two goals in mind. One of their goals is to speculate on the ebbs and flows of the price of the stock, regardless of which direction it's going to go in. Their second goal would be to limit their losses as much as possible. This was also something we discussed earlier on in the course. Attempting to protect your investments often comes at the cost of sacrificing the potential reward.

Chapter 4
Paper Trading Essentials

We have talked a lot about trying out your potential strategies by using one of those online simulators, but there is another way to see how a potential trade may pan out without putting up any capital. Paper trading has long since been a staple in options trading and with good reason before the rise of these online resources. So examine why this approach is so helpful, especially with these more complicated strategies.

Paper trading is pretty simple. Potential trades are written down on pieces of paper and then later recorded on a spreadsheet that details all of your positions, portfolios, profits, losses, and portfolios.

For a new investor to reap the most benefit from doing a little paper trading, formulating your investment plan and the opening and closing of positions should replicate actual trading guidelines and objectives. You, as the investor, should take the same risk-return objectives, investment constraints, and trading horizon into account as you would utilize with your actual brokerage account.

Another perk of going with paper trading is that the same strategy is able to be applied to a myriad market conditions, just to see under which conditions does your newly hewn strategy provides the best outcome. Let's look at a quick example: I set up a paper trade under market conditions that have high levels of volatility, and I know there are likely to be higher slippage costs due to more expansive spreads than compared to conditions that are moving in a mannerly fashion. If you remember, earlier slippage tends to crop up when an investor gets a much different price than the investor would expect from the time the trade is opened to the time the trade is exercised.

New investors and seasoned pros alike are able to use one of the simulated trading methods to get themselves familiar with the different order types.

One thing to keep in mind is that paper trading could give an investor a false sense of security and can give a distorted view of the expected returns you might achieve with your investment. Basically, what this slight warning boils down to is this, appearances may not match up with the real market because paper trading does not involve the risk investors feel when their cold hard cash is hanging out there on the line. Another thing is that paper trading gives you an inflated view of basic strategies, those like buying low and selling high, and these are some of the most challenging tenets to keep to in real life, but it is so much easier to keep your goals in mind while paper trading.

A harsh fact a lot of investors face is that they tend to experience a wide swath of emotions and judgment when real money is at stake, and this has the ability to make them display unusual behavior when working within the confines of a live account.

Pros of Paper Trading

Practice: perhaps the most important pro, in my humble opinion. You are able to gain experience in every aspect of the trading action, from the prep and research stages all the way to exercising the trade and recording a profit or loss. If you are working within the broker's simulator, there you are able to see how to utilize real money software while in a relaxed state of mind, which is good because becoming familiar and not being afraid to hit the wrong keystroke and accidentally trigger a full-scale disaster.

No-Risk: the solid point here is that paper trading costs nothing, and no matter what you do, you can't lose your capital by making a bad decision or jumping in and opening a trade at the most inopportune time. Paper trading also shows you all of the potential flaws in your analysis so you can begin the strenuous job of constructing a well-defined strategy.

Confidence: building your confidence in your investment skills and your ability to think on your feet, make snap decisions, and actually experience that rush of emotions when gaining your <u>hypothetical profits</u> can do great things in causing a new investor's confidence to grow in leaps and bounds so that they are able to do the same steps when your actual money is at stake.

No Stress: remember when we talked about one of the cons that people who decide to trade in options must get under control? Controlling your emotions of fear and greed is huge; losing your grip over these emotions tends to cloud the information necessary for helping mitigate your exposure to risk. By engaging in a little paper trading, you are able to pull those emotions out of the equation. Then you are better able to focus on the process and not the pitfalls.

Statistics: one of the benefits of paper-trading for a significant amount of time is the useful insights you can glean about your new strategy and how it functions within certain market conditions. The outcome might not be exactly what you want to see and might be discouraging, causing the new investor to want to proceed with their options education. This process might require additional paper trading rounds and compiling new data.

Limitations on Paper Trading

Emotional Actuality: this practice doesn't discuss or inspire emotions generally produced by actual profits or losses. In actual trading situations, a lot of investors cut their profits short and allow their losses to run wild because they lack the discipline to stick with their strategies. That self-destructive streak isn't so heavily weighted when dealing with hypothetical figures.

Formfitting: those who engage in paper trading always find their ideal entry and exit points, easily navigating the potential minefield produced by the computer-driven environment. These situations become too recognizable to real-world participants who have sat back and observed dozens of technically proven strategies go up in flames when market conditions shift into rough seas and attempt to nullify their <u>stops</u>.

Market Tie-In: another thing paper trading fails to take into account is the overall market's impact on single stocks. The greater amount of equities tends to flow in tandem with the major indices during times of extreme market correlation, which happens pretty regularly when the <u>Market Volatility Index </u>climbs. While results may look either really good, or really bad on paper, broader market conditions may have produced the outcome other than the virtues or failures of the singular position.

Slippage and Commissions: the issue investors don't think about when paper trading compared to real-life investing is that in an actual trading situation, there are all sorts of hidden costs from slippage and commissions to take into account. This fact is made worse by having wide spreads and those are generally not structured accurately in most paper trading situations. As a quick example, the contract you are purchasing at $50.00 could end up costing you $50.75 or more in an actual trading scenario.

Chapter 5

Everything LEAPS

We briefly went over LEAPS earlier in the course in very general terms, but in this chapter, we really want to dive into how this works and fits into your big-picture investment goals. So let's start with an easy one. The acronym breaks down to this basic definition, long-term equity anticipation securities, or LEAPS, as those in the financial sector call it. These are publicly-traded options contract that has an expiration date that is farther than a year out and generally is anywhere up to three years in the future. Basically, they are just like any other options contract except with the longer time period until the contract's end date.

With the longer time frame until maturity is a huge plus for those long-term investors. They are able to gain insight into prolonged price shifts in the market trends. Just like with any of the short-term contracts, an investor utilizing this strategy would still have to pay a fee for the ability to purchase or sell either above or below the strike price of the option.

One thing it is important to note with LEAPS is that the premiums tend to be higher than those for your basic options contract, even for the same exact underlying stock. That's because the longer you are out from the expiration date would give the underlying stock longer to make a tangible impact and for you to make a decent profit. This aspect is known as the time value, and investors use the prolonged timeframe and the IV of the contract in order to decide the value of the contract.

If you remember that the IV is an estimated value of how probable the option is to produce a profit based on the variance between the stock's market and strike price. The IV may encompass profit that is already included in the contract before it is purchased. The person writing the contract will utilize a thorough analysis of the underlying stock or sector to help assign the IV.

Of course, there are other things that have the potential to affect the premium price. These aspects can include volatility, interest rate, and if you are lucky enough to find the asset that returns dividends.

The last thing to keep in mind here is that during the life of the options contract, the contract will have value gleaned from utilizing different models and formulas. This wavering price demonstrates what the investor could receive if they decide to sell their option to another investor before the end date of the contract.

The innovative thing is that LEAPS will give investors access to the long-term options market, saving the investor from having to use a combination of shorter-term options to see the same result. Remember most short-term contracts are constructed with a maximum end date of a year. Without using LEAPS, if a potential investor wanted a two-year contract, they would have to purchase a year-long option, let it expire, then concurrently buy another 1-year contract.

This action, which is called rolling contracts over, would leave the investor unprotected in regards to market shifts in the underlying stock as well as accruing additional premiums. LEAPS can provide the long-term trader with exposure to a lengthy trend for a particular stock with one simple trade.

Types of LEAPS

Like any options contract, there are two major types, a put option, and a call option. By adding LEAPS, we open up a whole new level of an options contract, so what changes? Let's see it now.

Puts: if we are talking about puts in regards to how having LEAPS involved changes things, I think the major difference is that LEAPS puts give traders a long-term <u>hedge</u> if they have acquired the underlying security. Remember that a put <u>generally</u> gains in monetary value when an underlying security's price dips. This may offset the losses one might sustain if they own the stock shares. Essentially, the put may potentially help soften the blow of falling stock prices.

As a quick example here, I have an investor that owns shares of Microsoft and wishes to hang onto them for an extended term. This investor is a little fearful that the stock price might take a dip. To alleviate some of these concerns, I could advise the investor to purchase LEAPS puts on Microsoft in order to hedge against adverse moves one might run into with the <u>long</u> stock position. The reason why some investors love this strategy is because LEAPS puts assist investors in making sure they can benefit from price dips without having to short sell any shares of the underlying security.

The strategy of short selling consists of borrowing shares of an underlying security from a professional stockbroker and then selling them with the presumption that the stock will continue to take a nosedive by the expiration. On the expiration, the shares are bought, and you hope it's at a lower price, and the position is set up for either a significant gain or loss. One thing to remember here is that short selling might become extremely risky if the underlying stock price climbs instead of dropping, thus potentially creating significant losses.

Calls: LEAPS call options authorize the investor to profit from the potential upward momentum in an underlying stock, all the while utilizing less funding rather than buying the shares with cash upfront. This all works because the premium's fee is less than the capital necessary to purchase a hundred shares. You may recognize that there are some shared characteristics of short-term calls. The LEAPS call contracts give investors the ability to exercise their

options by buying the underlying stock at the strike
price.

Another advantage of these types of calls is
that they let the investor sell the option at any point
as long as it is before the end date. The variation in
the premium price that occurs between the purchase
and sale price can easily lead to a significant profit or
loss. Something else to consider is that the investor
needs to include any additional costs to buy or sell
the contract.

Advantages and Disadvantages of LEAPS

Did you honestly think that we wouldn't go into
the pros and cons of this strategy? We just switched
the wording this time to keep you on your toes. But
let's talk about some of these aspects so you can get
a good idea of what you can expect by using this
strategy.

Advantages

The longer time period involved with a LEAPS
contract grants you the ability to sell the option.

There is a myriad of LEAPS options out there in
the market for those investors who want to use

equity indices. This boils down to the fact you are able to hedge your contracts to protect your portfolio from experiencing any drastic changes in the market. An additional perk of using this strategy is that you can take a bearish or bullish stance on the market as an overarching big picture kind of thing instead of focusing so intently on the individual equities.

Another thing to keep in mind as an advantage is that the investor has the ability to use a LEAPS contract in order to shield your bets against variations in your overall portfolio.

The price for these contracts isn't as responsive to the changes in the underlying stock. If the price for the underlying stock changes, then the value of the contract won't necessarily make a big move all by itself.

Disadvantages

You could be vulnerable to adverse movements taking place in the market or even in individual companies. This aspect can somewhat affect your position.

The premiums you can expect to pay when dealing with LEAPS are a lot more expensive than some other types of investments.

Because you're investing your capital in a long-term plan, your money is locked up for the duration of the contract. This implies that if you come across another good investment opportunity, you might not be able to take advantage of it.

The price value for LEAPS seems to be highly reactive and is often subject to market changes and interest rate fluctuations.

Example

So, for the purpose of this example, let's just say that an investor client of mine possesses an extensive portfolio, the majority of which includes some of the S&P 500 heavy hitters. My client is nearly positive that there will end up being a major market turn-around later in the next two years and, therefore, purchases some LEAPS puts that are listed on the S&P 500. He does this in order to safeguard their portfolio against any adverse moves the market decides to make.

My client buys a December 2021 LEAPS option that has a strike of 3,000 on the S&P 500 and gives $300 upfront for the ability to sell the index shares at $3,000 when the end date of the contract rolls around.

If the index drops below 3,000 by the end date, the stock you currently hold in your portfolio will likely dip, but the LEAPS put would only rise in valuation, helping to offset any losses the portfolio might experience. But, if the S&P 500 climbs, the LEAPS put option will expire worthlessly, and then my client would be out their three-hundred dollar premium.

Chapter 6
The PERCS Are Endless

Another acronym that has a lot of power in regards to options is PERCS: Preference Equity Redemption Cumulative Stock and is an equity derivative that is defined as a hybrid security. The thing about this strategy is that it will automatically convert to equity when it reaches its pre-determined expiration date.

So, how does this all work? PERCS is what those in the financial sector would call a convertible preferred stock with an enhanced dividend, and it is limited in both term and participation. PERCS shares are able to be exchanged for shares of stock in the underlying company upon its expiration date. If the underlying shares are trading on a different wavelength after learning what the PERCS strike price is, then the shares will be exchanged at a rate of 1:1; but if the shares are trading higher than the strike price, these shares are only able to be exchanged up to the value of the strike price.

PERCS is essentially a covered call option and is attractive under conditions of yields in a state of decline because of the enhanced dividend involved. Upside profits tend to be limited in the interest of producing a higher yield. PERCS is typically cashed in before their end date, but usually, they are at a premium compared to whatever the cap price is. Generally, a nice rule of thumb is that if a holder of a PERCS contract does not redeem the shares within the required time frame, usually a three-to five-year period, the shares would undoubtedly be turned into common shares of stock. The dividends would return to regular dividends that one would expect to receive on shares of common stock.

We briefly mentioned this above, but as a quick definition, mandatory convertibles would-be stocks that possess their own distinctive list of risk and reward characteristics, but the thing that it's important to keep in mind is there all of them share basic features. These include a potential upside value that is typically less than the underlying stock. This is because convertible buyers are required to pay a premium just for the right to convert their shares and also for the higher rates on the enhanced dividends.

There are three main characteristics of PERCS.

They are required to have the ability to convert to an underlying stock.

They must possess a dividend yield that is more than that of the underlying security.

The investor is entitled to gain appreciation, but it is going to be limited especially compared to the potential level of appreciation of the underlying stock.

There are some other strategies like PERCS if you are interested in working this into your investment plan. All of these are definitely worth a Google search if you are interested in learning about some other new techniques:

Dividend Enhanced Convertible Stocks, also known as DECS

Automatically Convertible Equity Securities, also known as ACES.

Structured Yield Product Exchangeable For Stock, also known as STRYPES

Example

Let's say I own 10 PERCS on a boutique furniture chain, and there is a strike price of $50.

When these reach maturity one of the following outcomes might occur:

If once it reached the point of maturity, the underlying stock was rushing out the door at $40, I would receive a total of 10 common shares, and each of them is worth $40.

Or, once it hits maturity, the underlying stock traded at $100, I would obtain shares up to the overall value of the strike price of the PERCS, and, in this example, that would translate to be five shares that are worth about a hundred dollars apiece $100. This means the total value exchanged will equal the original strike of $50 x 10 shares.

Just for perspective, let's just say that the dividend handed out on the common shares comes out to be somewhere around $1.00 per year. The PERCS shares could potentially pay out a dividend of around $1.20 per year which is a pretty expansive diference between the two, in my opinion.

Chapter 7
What to Do When Things Get Messy?

We've talked a lot about what to do in order to solid up your financial strategy. We've introduced some new concepts, and talked about how to best make these work within the confines of the skills we have been discussing throughout the course up to this point, and now there are a few game plans that we need to go over. I call this part the safety valve. Do you know what to do in order to make the appropriate call given the market conditions? What about how to course correct? This chapter is like a catch-all. We are going to explore some new information on what to do when the markets are calm, and what to do when the storm is right outside the window and raging? We'll talk about everything from soup to nuts in this chapter. Let!s get started with one of my favorite topics. How to get ready to write a put option and sell it under any kind of market conditions.

In the moment when the market is in a state of decline, deciding to sell a put option can be an excellent idea. But here's the thing, if you make the decision to go this route, it is absolutely essential that you have the knowledge in place to know how to sell puts inside and out. Because when the price of a stock begins to fall, it tends to happen in the blink of an eye. The pacing and quick ebbs and flows often lead to an expansion of volatility in the markets, which as a side effect, increases the premiums of the option. This increase is entirely plausible because options tend to experience time decay, so a time with prices moving rapidly is the optimum condition that investors are looking for.

Going about selling these contracts when more volatility is present in the market insinuates that investors will net a higher return thanks to the increased cost of the premiums. Seasoned traders like to sell puts in aspirations of being able to bank the money from the premium. Nevertheless, those who like to invest for the long haul should consider selling puts as a way to purchase shares in companies or sectors that they regard at a lower cost. The Godfather of investing, Warren Buffett, has utilized many strategies just like that one in the past.

Those in the financial sector always say that the most opportune time to purchase stocks is the time when the markets are in decline. But a lot of traders simply don't have the emotional bandwidth to handle the risk associated. Branching out and selling a put contract is just one of a thousand ways to take the edge off and reduce your stress.

Examples

How about we work out a quick example here. Let's say I'm a fan of Mavi, a new tech company, I want to get involved and invest, but I'm still really unsure about how the market is going to act. Ideally, I want to have 500 shares. With the current stock price of $50, buying that many shares would end up costing me somewhere in the neighborhood of $25,000. But there's a loophole, and I could sell five puts. Let's just say I decided to sell next month's $45 put options on Mavi for three bucks.

When I do so, I will bank $1,500 from the premium I received from the sale. With this example, I'm not factoring in commissions because a lot of brokerages allow you to trade with no commission, or they are usually pretty low, but if we want to take a look at how the commission might shake out let's, break this down. Since I wrote the option, I have to buy 500 shares of Mavi at any time before the end date for $45. If I have to buy the stock, my net cost without paying commission would be $42 a share because of the option premium.

So since I'm not buying the 500 shares outright and instead just selling the put, I went from plopping down my $25,000 to purchase the shares to now, I'm collecting $1,500 in premiums. But here's what you want to pay attention to, if Mavi's stock price dips below that $45 threshold, then I would have the stock "put" on my shoulders. But, my cost for the shares would be $22,500 minus the $1,500 I had already collected in premiums.

You have already learnt this, but it bears repeating... deciding to sell puts isn't a foolproof strategy. There is always something that might potentially go wrong. For example, if my Mavi shares or any company that you sell options on really take a significant nosedive, you would potentially still be hatching your losses. The premiums you collect will just shrink the losses, but it won't completely mitigate them. On the other hand, what would potentially happen if the stock price continued to rise. Then, the investor would potentially miss out on further profits that could have been achieved beyond just the option premium.

So in the example above it really targets your approach to working with some difficult market conditions. With this next example of selling a put call, we are going to break down a more prudent approach to working with a put call.

Let's look at another example. Suppose that Amazon is thrilling investors with increasing profits after they introduced a new, revolutionary product. Amazon's stock is trading at $270, and your price-to-earnings ratio shows a reasonable value for this company's fast growth. I'm feeling bullish about the prospects I'm seeing. I notice that I was able to buy 100 shares for $27,000, plus commissions and fees.

In this situation, I decide I want to sell a January $250 put that will expire two years today, and it will be priced at $30. If you remember our discussion on expiration dates and when trades settle, this would mean that the put will expire on the third Friday of January in 2024. It also has an exercise price of $250. One contract covers 100 shares. As we have discussed countless times, so by this logic, this would allow me to collect $3,000 in premiums upfront.

By deciding to sell the option, I'm signing a contract and pledge to purchase a hundred shares of Amazon for $250 a share, and I am locked into doing this no later than January 2024. Understandably, since Amazon shares are trading around $270 dollars today, the buyer isn't going to sell me the shares for $250, which is $20 below the current market price, and therefore they aren't stupid; it's a smart plan. So I'll collect the premium while we wait.

Now, if the stock drops to $250 before the expiration date rolls around in January two years from now, I'll be required to buy the shares at that price. But the good news is that I get to keep the $30 premium per share. With that, my cost will come out to around $220 for each share. However, if the price never dips to $250, the option will meet its expiration date and be considered worthless, and I would get to keep the entire $3,000 dollar premium that I received.

Taking this a step further, as a plan B, instead of purchasing a hundred shares for $27,000, I could see both of my open positions and lower my cost to $220 per share, or a total of $22,000 for 100 shares, if the price falls to $250 per share. But, if the option expires worthless, I will get to keep the $30 premium assessed on each share, which equates to a 12% return on a $250 per share price.

It can be a distinctive plan to sell puts on stocks you would like to own. If Amazon declines, I would have to pay somewhere in the neighborhood of $25,000 in order to purchase the shares at $250. If you banked that $3,000 premium, my net cost would be $22,000. It's something that you might want to keep in mind that if you have a full-service broker, they have the ability to force you to leverage other holdings in order to buy this position if you don't have the available cash sitting in your brokerage account.

Chapter 8
Iron Condor Has Landed

In this chapter, we will be detailing one of the more complicated options strategies as a precursor to featuring our advanced strategies in the last section of the course. While it has a super cool/intimidating name, once you get the hang of how this strategy works and its optimal applications, it's not too hard to understand where it fits with your financial toolbox.

Many seasoned traders are clamoring for more defined-risk, high-probability options. Those actively engaged in the markets understand that it's impractical to expect every trade to be profitable. But looking for favorable outcomes and keeping an eye on your level of risk management is a great help in orchestrating a winning strategy.

We have discussed the merits of a vertical credit spread before and how they are fairly versatile when you want to take a directional stance. Selling a vertical spread on a put would be what most people consider a bullish trade. On the other side, if you sold a vertical spread call, that would be considered a bearish trade. Plus, when you are selling verticals, the risk is already pretty well-defined: It's restricted to whatever the width of the long and short prices minus the premium collected but then you have to subtract any transaction costs incurred. Here's the fun part. What happens if your perspective is neutral, or if the underlying security seems mired in a turbulent market? Well, then we'll need to call in the <u>iron condor</u>.

This strategy is defined by combining an out-of-the-money short put spread and an OTM short call spread using contracts that all expire on the same date.

But what are the best strike prices traders typically want to utilize for the two spreads? Deciding what the strike should be in terms of an iron condor may take a little getting used to. Some investors choose to pick some prices at random, or you can factor in a little bit of variety, throw in some super special trader math, and come up with a couple of potential prices for you to use in your options strategy. This doesn't automatically mean that you'll have an easy and successful trade, but at least you'll have a solid script to work from.

Here's some food for thought: when you decide to get rid of two separate OTM vertical spreads, that means collecting the premiums on both sides of the iron condor as one order. But the market can't be helping out at two arenas at once. So once you make it to the final date, only one vertical can go against you.

The great part about this is how it sounds like you can bring in the premium for two separate spreads without increasing the level of risk you have exposed yourself to, right? Well, kind of. Let's look at an example to help break this down.

Example

For this example, let's say that a underlying security is currently trading at $112 and a client of mine decides they want to sell the 110-105 put spread and the 115-120 call spread. This particular setup would create the iron condor, for a credit of $2.59. The maximum risk level you face on either spread is $5 – $2.59 or $2.41 per spread. This amounts to $241 with a one-contract spread, not factoring in any other transaction costs.

If the underlying security stays above $110 or dips below $115 until their respective expiration dates, then both spreads should expire worthlessly, and my client will be able to keep the $259 profit per spread as the profit.

It is important to take note that after setting up a short option, it could be fulfilled by the investor at any time leading up to expiration, regardless of the ITM amount.

Yes, the maximum amount my client could potentially lose is somewhere in the neighborhood of $241 for either leg of the spread, so they hadn't increased their risk by deciding to sell both spreads. But they had increased the exposure to lose in terms of where the market could potentially go in order for that loss to occur. For example, if my client had sold only the put spread potion of the iron condor, as long as the stock traded above the $110 threshold up til the end date, the spread should expire worthlessly. Then it wouldn't be a concern as to how high the stock climbed above that point.

On the other hand, if the investor sold only the call spread, the stock could keep bottoming out; as long as it traded below $115 through the last day of the contract, the call spread should expire worthlessly.

The main benefit of this plan depends on the market trading within a specific price range. That's where strike selection becomes such an important part of the strategy. One thing it might be wise to keep in mind is that hanging onto your positions all the way up to their expiration can warrant additional risks; one thing that might happen is something like an unanticipated event could occur, or an anticipated event may fail to occur. Both could potentially lead to a wildly different outcome than what you might have expected when you first started out.

Since the iron condor is a defined strategy, an investor could potentially take advantage of increased premiums leading up to the release of a company's earnings report. The uncertainty surrounding the release of such information can sometimes mean that volatility will begin to creep up to higher levels. The premium one might expect to glean from an options contract, could inflate the values of the specific vertical spreads. So the money you pick up when trading while utilizing an iron condor could be better. At the same time, it's also not the worst thing.

An investor could also decide to utilize a short iron condor strategy in order to take advantage of the higher premiums built on the following assumptions:

Volatility is inching higher but might level out after the earnings report is released.

The underlying stock's value will be somewhere in the middle of the two strike prices of the iron condor after the report is released. (It's obvious to see the risk in this assumption, and some investors might view the same underlying stock in the opposite way and assume that the stock will experience a significant price jump upon the release of the earnings report.

Selecting the correct strike price to be used in an iron condor strategy by utilizing a certain mathematical or fundamental formula may be wiser than shooting in the dark and picking what you want your strike value to be. However, it doesn't mean the trade can't falter if the stock price climbs or dips to a level further than the expected range one would expect to see prior to or at expiration.

These kinds of strategies are all about trade-offs. Basically, it all boils down to your objectives and goals.

Chapter 9
Broken Wing Butterfly

I'm Not Making These Names Up

A butterfly spread is a top-tier strategy among seasoned options traders who predict that the price of an underlying security to be comparable to the butterfly's short strike price upon its expiration date. The butterfly spread is typically constructed as a debit, which basically just means that you will be paying a net premium to open the position.

Here's a quick look at what the butterfly spread is and how it relates to the strategy we just discussed in the last chapter.

The basic definition of a butterfly spread helps away a lot of the confusion. Basically, it is just the sale of two options at the same strike price and the purchase of 2 contracts of the same type, but one will have a higher price, and the other will be at the opposite end of the spectrum. And if you flip back and take a look at how the iron condor is structured, you'll be able to see that utilizing this strategy is akin to selling an iron condor.

But if you make one teensy little change to the butterfly, you will transform an already solid strategy into a really exciting prospect, an unbalanced, or as it is commonly known as a broken wing, butterfly. This new strategy produces a brand-new risk profile. If you build this from the ground up, this spread can be opened at a credit, which we all like because that means you receive a premium right off the bat.

For these examples, let's just say, for simplicity's sake, that the underlying security is currently trading at $70, and the call options chain might look something like this:

Call Strike	Call Bid	Call Ask
75	$1.65	$1.70
80	$1.10	$1.15
85	$0.65	$0.75
90	$0.30	$0.35

Figure 30: Butterfly spread

Let's start off by deciding we are going to use a butterfly spread and with the underlying stock I'm looking at right now. I think calls are going to be my best bet. Using the values listed in the graphic on the previous page, you could buy the $75-$80-$85 butterfly call by buying one each of the $75 and $85 calls, which would make them the wings at the asking price, and getting rid of two of the $80 calls, deemed the body at the bid price. With the stock trading around $70, this spread would end up with the total cost $1.70 + $0.70 – (2 x $1.10) = $0.20.

The maximum profit for the butterfly spread would be if the stock eventually settled at $80 when we reach the expiration. The $75-strike call would, potentially, be worth five dollars, and the rest of the contract would expire worthless, which leaves you with a potential profit of ($5.00 – $0.20 x 100) = $480. And I bet you are wondering about the maximum loss? If the underlying stock falls on either side of the wings, below the $75 threshold or above the $85 threshold, then you will be out the initial debit of $20. Something important to note here is that short options traditionally have the ability to be allocated at any time up until expiration. This regardless of being ITM or not.

Unbalancing the Wings

The thing with this strategy is that if you're at ease with a stock position, or maybe even the risk associated with getting into a stock position, then that's great! Feeling confident in your investment plan is what we have been working toward ever since we started this course. But for a quick example, what would you do if the underlying stock is hovering around the 80-strike and the option is about to expire, the caveat is that. you might not know if you've been assigned until after the close, so you have to wait with bated breath until morning in order to double-check and potentially have to cover your position if the situation calls for it. Some investors decide to unravel these types of positions before the expiration date rolls around in order to avoid these risks.

So, it might be necessary to make one little adjustment to help you rest easy with utilizing this strategy. Let's just say that you wanted to open the spread as a credit instead of a debit. One way to proceed in this way is to choose a higher and less expensive strike price for that last aspect of the spread. By making this slight change, the strategy may then allow you to gather a premium when you open the position, but the only downside is that it will also bring more potential risk right to your front door.

Let's take another look at the values we have in the table on the previous page. Let's just that instead of purchasing the $85-strike call for $0.70 for use as the far wing of the strategy, you purchased the $90-strike call at $0.35. It's cheaper, so it should be better, right? This change would turn the trade into a $75-$80-$90 broken wing butterfly. Instead of paying $0.20 for the butterfly spread like in the previous example, in this situation, you would receive $0.15 x 100 = $15.

For this example, we need to look at every angle, so if the stock trades below $75 at its end date, instead of you throwing away the price paid when you opened the position, you would get to maintain the premium you were paid. This is exactly why some investors decide to utilize a broken wing butterfly as a substitute for an OTM vertical credit spread. But, where this strategy differs from a credit spread is where the max profit potential is limited to the entry value. By using this strategy, you would retain the profit of the regular butterfly. So in this situation, for instance, if the stock settles at $80 at expiration, the maximum profit of this strategy is essentially $5 plus the entry credit of $0.15, or $515 with the multiplier, if it comes into play.

As you progress through setting up your strategy, don't miss out on going through and examining the what-if expiration case studies like in the example above. However, this time use the 90-strike so there are no surprises that may crop up during and after the expiration date. Remember, this strategy is one of the more advanced you might find yourself getting into, so it seems a little intimidating, but it will get easier.

Now, getting back to our example, when you approach breaking off or potentially unbalancing that particular wing can deliver something you might not want to think of: risk exposure. Since you're adjusting the wing and sending it further OTM, you are substantially increasing your risk exposure. With every dollar you adjust the wing further from where you started, you raise the risk potential by $1 or $100 with the multiplier in place. Let's see how that looks in this example. Moving the topmost wing from the $85-strike call to the $90-strike adds an additional five hundred dollars of risk, and you know I like to check and see what my worst-case scenario is going to look like so I can adequately prepare if need be, so after we run the numbers, the trade would result in this, ($500 − $0.15 initial credit) = $485.

One more thing to not forget is that a debit butterfly, if the wings are set at equal distances, will usually require no additional margin. So, in essence...if you break a wing or skip over a strike, then this strategy would be considered a debit spread and a credit spread, and you'd probably have to post some additional margin.

After teaching this strategy, the first question a lot of my clients as is a good one. It bears some merit for us to stop for a minute and think about this one. The question becomes, is breaking the wing just for extra credit worth the additional risk you may expose yourself to? To me, it depends on your outlook, the simplest answer I give my clients is that no one can answer that question quite as they can, and it is up to each particular investor to decide what works best for them.

Some investors would arrange the middle strike price of their broken wing at the farthest end of the range they are shooting for with the underlying stock. If that happens, it would require a larger-than-life type of move to get the stock in that "danger zone." But if it does, then it might make it worth it to cut your losses and close out of the trade earlier than you might want to.

The last thought I want to impart as we prepare to move on is this. Broken wing butterflies aren't a slam dunk or even appealing to every trader, every market, or for every level of implied volatility. But having a solid idea of how things are structured and the functions of the strategy can often be a good first step in ascertaining if this strategy is right for you and your investment plan and goals.

Chapter 10
Honorable Mention
Strategies

We are finishing up this section of the course with an honorable mention strategy chapter. These strategies and examples are considered a little more advanced than some of the ones we began the course discussing. As we have built upon our knowledge, it hopefully makes it seem like these aren't quite as daunting as they might be when you are first doing a Google search because you are trying to gauge your own interest in getting involved in trading. With these strategies being a little more complicated, it may seem like they aren't for an investor that has less than 2-3 years in the financial sector. However, I want you to be able to see that the information for any strategy you might see is right there at your fingertips. If you hear about some cool-sounding strategy that sounds like its concepts and what it accomplishes would line up with your investment goals, then let's take a look at it! With options the sky is the limit, that's not to say go out there, and with your first trade right off the bat, you are exercising the most advanced strategy that even Mr. Buffett himself would kind of side-eye skeptically. Do your homework, lay your foundation by diving deep into your research, then engage in a little back testing or paper trading in order to see how your strategy is going to pan out. Now, let's get to our shortlist of strategies and spreads that you might want to consider adding to your financial toolbox.

The Synthetic Long Stock

This strategy basically is composed of purchasing a call and then selling a put in the same month, and they both have the same strike price. The trader who opens this strategy will be purchasing the stock at the first strike; price A in the graphic on the next page if they decide they will want to hold the position until expiration. If the stock price climbs above where price A is, then the trader probably will want to issue the call option, but if the stock dips below price A the trader will be assigned the put. Essentially you are going to end up owning the stock at price A, one way or another. Sounds okay so far right? Well, sort of...there's a bit more to it that you should be aware of before just jumping in the deep end with both feet.

The one aspect of this strategy I really want you to hone in on is that the position strongly resembles that of a long stock position. With those, as we have touched upon before this point, most investors don't really want to hang onto that particular position until the end date comes to pass.

One of the pros of this strategy is that the profit potential is basically unlimited since owning the stock would allow the trader the ability to keep raking in the money as the stock continues to climb. This is both a good and bad thing in my book, we know there will always be a downtrend as far as the underlying securities go, they won't always continue to climb, and eventually, they will always fall.

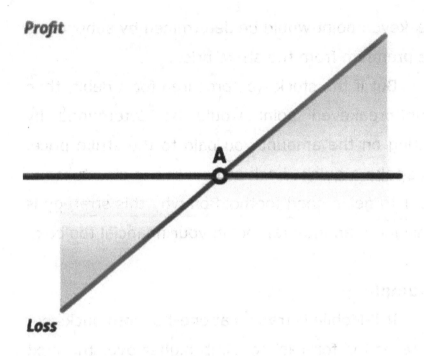

Figure 31: Synthetic long stock

But with the higher profit potential, the loss is also unlimited, or at least until it hits rock bottom at zero. The thing to remember here is that as the stock dips in price, your losses will continue to pile up.

This strategy has just one breakeven point, but that point is calculated in varied ways contingent on if the synthetic long stock was obtained for a credit or a debit.

If the stock was obtained for credit, then your

breakeven point would be determined by subtracting the premium from the strike price.

But if the stock was procured for a debit, then your breakeven point would be determined by putting on the amount you paid to the strike price. Let's take a quick check at how this is structured in order to get a good foothold on why this strategy is considered an integral tool in your financial toolbox.

Example

If T-Mobile is trading at one-hundred bucks per share and is forecast to climb higher over the next three months, an investor could purchase a $100-strike call and sell a $100-strike price put for the following values:

Buy 1 T-Mobile 100-strike call for $4.00

Sell 1 T-Mobile 100-strike put for $3.50

The net premium = $0.50 debit

For the purposes of this example, the stock has climbed to $105 on the expiration date of the contract; therefore, the investor will acquire $5.00 on the underlying stock, but because they spent fifty cents on the synthetic long stock, they end up with a net gain of $4.50.

But let's look at what happens to our numbers if the stock dips and ends up at $95 upon its expiration. In that case, the investor would be assigned a $100-strike put, purchasing the stock for $100. This basically means that they sustained a $5.00 loss on the put, but since they purchased the synthetic long stock for fifty cents, they would end up with a total loss of $5.50.

Risk Reversal

The next strategy we are going to break down is the risk reversal strategy. This one is a strategy I personally use quite often, and it's an important one for you to consider adding to your rotation on the strategies you can pull out and slide into place without a lot of shenanigans taking place. Let's start with the basic definition of what this is and how it works.

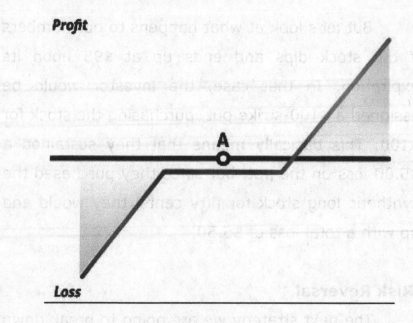

Figure 32: Risk reversal

This particular strategy works by purchasing an OTM call option and selling an OTM put option within the same expiration month. A lot of investors and experts will mention that this is considered a pretty bullish strategy, and it is one that is able to be turned into either a debit or a credit, much like the strategy we just finished discussing, depending on where the strike prices are in comparison to the underlying stock price.

The trader who jumps into this strategy wants

to reap the benefit from being long on the call contract but wants to be able to pay for the call by selling the put. I like this one for that very reason, but as we are going to discuss in a minute, there are some potential pitfalls to where, if you are not paying attention, your trade could potentially hit quite the speed bump. With a trade structured like this, it minimizes the chance of the underlying stock going sideways on you, but it does contain a substantial exposure to risk if the stock suddenly dips down.

This strategy has the polar opposite outcome than that of a collar strategy. With this strategy, it is constructed with the ability to protect a trader who is short on the underlying stock from an ascending stock price. If the trader is troubled about the price of a short stock position suddenly trending higher, they are always able to purchase an upside call and then pay for their trade by selling a downside put. This is the part you will need to remember, the trade needs to be executed on a 1:1 basis, or for every hundred shares the trader is short, the investor should open one risk reversal contract. This way it's a double-edged sword, so if the stock climbs, then the trader would be safeguarded by the upside long call option. And if the stock just so happened to be traded at a lower point, then the traded would be required to purchase the stock at the short put's lower price point.

This strategy is also able to be used in an aggressive bull trade, we briefly alluded to this earlier, but the question becomes why? The reason behind this is that the trader is purchasing a higher strike call option and arranging for the premium to be paid by selling an OTM put option. The investor is basically embarking upon a bull trade for almost no cost or even acquiring a credit. If the trader's hunch is right, and the stock continues to climb toward the heavens, then the short put will become worthless, and the long call would increase in value. Giving the investor a substantial profit.

But here is the one caveat, if the trader is imprecise regarding the movement of the stock, they will be required to purchase the stock at the short put strike. Although this is pretty risky and could potentially generate significant losses. Being required to purchase the stock at a lower price point than the spot where the trader decided to open the risk reversal would end up with a better result than if the trader would've bought the stock right from the start.

Your profit potential is really considered unlimited as keeping a long position on an upside call allowed the investor to keep bringing in the profits as long as the underlying stock trends higher.

One thing to keep in mind the loss potential is also unlimited, at least until the underlying security drops in price. At that point, the losses continue to pile up upon the short put.

With this strategy, there is a single breakeven, but this point is determined differently and is dependent on if the risk reversal was opened as a credit or a debit.

If the strategy was acquired as credit, then your breakeven would be determined by taking the premium acquired from the strike price of the put.

If reversal was acquired as a debit, then your breakeven would be determined by adding the amount paid to whatever the call's strike price was.

Example

If Sony is trading at a hundred dollars per share and is forecasted to trade for more over the next year, an investor would be able to purchase a 120-strike call and sell an 80-strike put for the following values:

Purchase 1 Sony $120-strike call for $6.00

Sell 1 Sony $100-strike put for $7.00

Total premium = $1.00 credit

Now, we see that the stock is going for up to $105 upon its expiration date, so the investor will experience a zero gain on this trade since the stock has not made it to the strike price. However, since the trader banked a $1.00 credit on the reversal, the investor will receive a total profit of $1.00.

Now if the stock makes it to $130 upon expiration, the trader will have a $10.00 profit on the call since the stock has risen above the 120-strike price by $10. But, because they received a $1.00 credit for the reversal, then the trader will bank a total gain of $11.00.

But if the stock falls to $70 upon expiration, then the investor will be assigned the 80-put, being required to buy the stock for $80. In this situation then it would mean that they sustained a $10.00 loss on the put. However, since they received a credit of a dollar for the reversal, there would be a total loss of $9.00.

Christmas Comes Early

When I first started in options I spotted the name of this strategy, and I was laughing on the inside. I first thought "this has to be some kind of joke...how helpful is this going to be for my investment goal? I'm not Hallmark here." But come to find out, it is pretty helpful, but it does get a little complicated.

This call strategy is considered pretty advanced because of how it is structured, it is formatted with three legs in total, and there are six options contracts involved. I think the graphic on the next page will help us take this into sections so we can make sure we don't get lost.

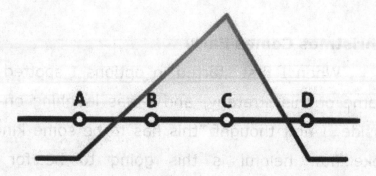

Figure 33: Christmas comes early

The option strategy consists of purchasing one call at strike A, leaping past strike B, then selling off three calls at strike C, and finally purchasing two other calls at strike D. I know what you are thinking, this spread looks a lot like a butterfly spread, and the necessary outcome, if everything falls into place correctly, is a pin located at the short middle strikes, but allows for a little more wiggle room on the upside. Therefore this is considered one of the more bullish strategies.

The price is also quite a bit higher than finding a way compared to that of a butterfly spread because of the long lower-legged strike that is furthest away from the short middle strikes. Since this position is exercised at a higher cost, the underlying security must take great strides in order to become successful. Although this strategy does contain a higher likelihood of sustaining a loss, a safety valve built into the spread is that in the event the stock does move in a direction unforeseen and against the investor, the potential losses are already capped at the opening price.

Your profit potential is set up by grabbing the difference between the lowest strike and the three short middle call strike prices, then subtracting the cost of the trade. So just quickly running the numbers here. If the range between points A and C was $10 and the trade cost $2.50, then your maximum profit would come out to be $7.50.

Your maximum loss, however, would be determined by the cost of the trade, so using the same example, your maximum loss would come out to be around $2.50.

With this spread, there are two breakeven

points automatically built-in. The lower breakeven is easily determined by taking the value for strike A and then adding the cost of the trade. So if strike A was a $90-strike option, and the trade cost $2.50, your lower breakeven would be $92.50.

The upper breakeven point would be revealed after taking the highest strike price, strike D in this case, and then subtracting half of the net debit. So, if strike D was equal to $105 and the cost of the trade was $2.50, then the upper breakeven would come out to be $103.75 (105-2.50/2).

Example

Let's work out this last example in the honorable mention strategies, so let's say that Panasonic is currently trading at $90 per share and is forecast to trade for more money during the course of the next three months. An investor could decide to utilize a 90/100/105 Christmas tree spread by purchasing one 90-strike call, selling three 100-strike calls, and purchasing two 105-strike price calls for the following values:

Buy one Panasonic $90-strike call for $8.00

Sell three Panasonic $100-strike calls for $6.90

total or $2.30 each.

Buy two Panasonic $105-strike calls for $1.40 or $.70 apiece

Grand total = $2.50

Now if the underlying stock trends downward during the next three months, the trader will have sacrificed the full $2.50, and all contracts will be eradicated from his account.

But if the stock trends upward and hits a hundred dollars upon its expiration date, then the investor would profit $10 on the movement of the underlying stock, thereby capitalizing with the $90-strike option. Simultaneously, the rest of the options on the spread will expire completely worthless. Since the investor paid $2.50 for the trade, the entire profit would come out to be somewhere in the neighborhood of $7.50.

Now, if the stock made its way to $110, the trader would gain $20 on the $90 call. They would love $10 for each of the three short middle $100-calls, which gives us a total of $30. They would profit $5 X2 on the long upper $105-calls, which gives us a total of $10.

So after some quick calculations, the result

would be $20 − $30 + $10, which shows us that all profits are a wash, but since the investor only paid $2.50 for the trade, the net loss they sustained is only $2.50.

Final Thoughts

As you can see with these three honorable mention strategies, each one has a very defined use and purpose. Make sure you select just the right strategy for your game plan; whether they are complicated/non-complicated, it doesn't matter. All that matters is what you feel comfortable wielding. If you aren't confident in how a strategy works or how it may react under certain market conditions, remember you can always engage in some backtesting or paper trading to let you get used to all of the moving parts before putting money on the line.

With these strategies, as well as those we have discussed at other points in the course, you already have a strong foothold in options trading. You have worked with some of the more commonly used strategies that have been called a road map to success. Now all that's left is to start putting things into practice.

Conclusion

With that closing chapter, we have made it successfully made it through section 5, and we have just one more section of this crash course in options trading to go. There is a lot of heavy material in this section that you might want to go back and read through again. I know with like the long condor, and the Christmas tree spread, it took me a few times of reading through all the steps and what were the benefits of each strategy.

There were a lot of legitimate questions I had about things, the more complicated things got. It's just part of learning to invest. No one has all the answers you may hope o find in one place, nor does anyone spring from the womb a perfectly coiffed stockbroker In an impeccably tailored Armani suit with a cappuccino in one hand and a smartphone firmly clasped in the other.

Devotion to the art of investing doesn't just happen overnight. This drive to invest is an integral part of some people's lives. Their entire day and schedule revolve around the markets and the opening and closing bell. It revolves around the constant hunger for more information, whether it's company or sector-specific, or if it is just researching and trying out new strategies. Never lose that desire to constantly be bettering yourself, making your investment plan impenetrable to outside influences.

Your time is now, and it's about time for me to release you out into the world of investing with just the air beneath you holding yourself up... as we embark on this last section, let me impart a few words of wisdom. You've got this! Investing is certainly not for everyone, and if you have been committed and made it this far, there is nothing you cannot accomplish. Your trades are going in a solid direction. I know already because I helped you lay the groundwork.

That's not to say I am an oracle, but it's just putting into practice what I've learned during the many years I've spent putting my blood, sweat, and tears into formulating my plan and working toward my goals.

Options Trading FAQ's

What are the benefits of trading options?

1.Options offer great leverage. You are able to control 100 shares of stock for a few hundred dollars or less.

2.Options can allow us to make money in many types of market conditions. Even then stocks are moving sideways.

3.There are options trades that can allows us to make money 5 different ways.

4.Trading options can be done in as little as 10 minutes a day.

5.Options trading allows us to control our risk better

than any other financial instrument out There

What options broker is best to use? While there are many options brokers available these days, there are two that we recommend above the rest.

The first is TastyWorks (https://www.tastyworks.com) and TD Ameritrade (https://www.tdameritrade.com). Both of these brokers offer great platforms with low commission rates. For those of you with busy schedules that like to trade from a mobile platform, both of these brokers also provide mobile apps to trade from. The benefit of TastyWorks is they offer a flat $1 per contract commission for an options trade. They also don't charge a closing commission so you will only be paying to enter the trade. They also cap their commissions at $10 per trade ($10 per leg on a spread). This can lead to big savings if you are trading bigger position sizes. Finally, TastyWorks doesn't have different levels of accounts like most other brokers. If you open an account with them you can trade any options strategy you want (long calls and puts as well as spreads). For these reasons, TastyWorks is our broker of choice.

Should I open a margin or cash account? We prefer using a margin account as it will allow us to trade vertical spreads. While you can open a cash account with less capital, you will be limited to buying calls and puts. This will greatly limit your flexibility in different market conditions. Most brokers require a $3,000 starting account size to open a margin account. Cash accounts can be opened with as little as $50.

What is the pattern day trading rule (PDT) and who does it apply to? Margin accounts under $25,000 are subject to the pattern day trading rule. This rule limits the number of day trades you can take. You are allowed 3 day trades in a 5 day stretch. Cash accounts are not subject to this rule. If you plan on day trading options with an account size less than $25,000 you will be better off with a cash account. How much capital should I start trading with? We recommend starting with a minimum of $3,500. While you can start with less than this it becomes much more difficult to control the risk if you do. Ideally, we want the risk to be kept to 2-5% of your account per trade.

Should I day trade or swing trade options? We find it much easier to swing trade options. We classify a swing trade as holding a position for anywhere from 2 days on out to 3 weeks. Day trading options can be difficult as it takes more time on a daily basis and also becomes less forgiving if the stock doesn't move in your favor immediately.

Which options strategy is best? The beauty of options trading is the flexibility that they offer as they allow us to do things that can't be done with any other financial instrument. The 3 strategies that we recommend all options traders use are: • long calls and puts • debit spreads • credit spreads We cover these strategies in detail including step by step criteria for each trade type in the free Options Trading For Income Crash Course which you will find links to above.

Is volume or open interest more important when trading options? Liquidity is a very important topic when trading options. The more active the options are the easier it will be to get filled on trades and at good prices. Volume indicates the number of contracts traded that day. Open interest will tell you the total number of option contracts that are outstanding. These are contracts that have been traded but have not been closed by an offsetting trade or an exercise or assignment. Unlike trading volume, open interest is not updated during the trading day. Ideally, we like to see good volume and open interest in the options that we trade. However, open interest is more important to us as it indicates those options have been active over a period of days. This will typically lead to tighter bid/ask spreads on the options, which means we will be able to get in and out of our trades at better prices.

Are weekly or monthly options best to trade?
We prefer to use options that have between 20-60 days left to expiration. This could be a mix of weekly options that have at least 20 days left to expiration along with monthly options. We find the monthly options easier to trade in most cases as they will have better liquidity meaning the volume and open interest are higher. We are open to trading the shorter duration options but like to see the VIX in the upper teens or low twenties when

doing so.

Should I trade In the Money or Out Of The Money options? While the out of the money options are attractive due to being cheaper, we much prefer trading the in the money options. They provide a higher quality position which will increase your odds of success. The out of the money options are cheap for a reason because they have a lower probability of success as there are more factors working against them. When buying options, we prefer to buy the options that are 1-2 strikes in the money from the entry point on your chart. This will give us the most bang for our buck. Stock movement vs Implied volatility vs Time decay All 3 of these can have a big impact on the prices of an option. When buying options, you need a big enough directional move in the stock in your favor and it has to happen quickly enough to offset the time decay and potential movement in volatility. I'm not opposed to buying options, but you need a lot to go right in your favor to make money. If the stock doesn't move fast enough or volatility drops too much while you are in the trade, you won't be as profitable. Trading credit spreads allows you to put on a trade where you are benefiting from time decay adding up and volatility decreasing. You are able to stack the deck in your favor by placing a trade that has 5 ways of making money. Stock movement, implied volatility, and time decay are all crucial factors to take into consideration when placing an options trade. Ignoring one of these factors can lead to very inconsistent returns over time. We talk about this in more detail in our free Options Trading For Income Crash Course at the links to above. Should,

I use limit or market orders when placing my trades? We highly recommend using limit orders when placing your options trades. When you use market orders you lose control over where you get filled at. This can lead to giving up too much on the fill prices. Market orders should only be used as a last resort option. When using limit orders, we like to place the orders at the mid price between the bid and ask prices. While this doesn't guarantee you will get filled on a trade at these prices, it's a good place to start. If you are placing a buy order and can't get filled at the mid price then you can adjust the order price higher by a few pennies.